STUMPED

Conundrums and Frivolous Questions by Ed Kaiser

Randall, I need answers

© Ed Kaiser 2018
978-0-9998096-2-4

Copyright © 2018 Ed Kaiser

All rights reserved. No part of this book may be reproduced or transmitted in any form or by any means, electronic or mechanical, including photocopying, recording, by any information storage and retrieval system, without permission in writing from the publisher.

ISBN 978-0-9998096-2-4
Printed in the USA

Cover and book design:
Marie Kar, Red Frame Creative

Published by Buttonwood Press, LLC
P.O. Box 716, Haslett, Michigan 48840
www.buttonwoodpress.com

Foreword

by Richard Baldwin

The English language is FUN. In some respects, it is laughable. The words we say and hear carry with them a variety of meanings. As a former teacher of profoundly hearing impaired children I was often at a loss to explain how one word had so many meanings. "Spring" can be a season, an action, a coil, or moving water. Many words depend on context clues which are provided by other words. Example: "April is a month in Spring."

This is why when I was introduced to Ed's Questions of the Day I found each question fun to reason and even more fun to try and answer. Tyler Hoag, a teenage friend of Ed's, after reading a sample of questions offered his own, "Why isn't "Chili" called "Hottie"?

Have fun with this set of questions and/or answers. Share with family and friends. See who is most creative in providing an answer. Make up your own.

Additional Questions can be found in Ed's three books: *Laughing at Life*, *Laughing in Stitches*, and *Laughing While Shopping*.

These books can be ordered from:

www.ButtonwoodPress.com
www.Amazon.com

Please help us with material for a follow up book. Send your creative question to Buttonwood Press LLC, P.O. Box 716, Haslett, Michigan 48840. Please include your name and address. These must be created by you and not lifted from copyright material.

Preface

I'm quite sure my mind is predisposed to observing normal, everyday things as mysterious. Most folks see a sign that proclaims **FRESH EGGS** and contemplate whether to buy or not. I wonder what other kind of eggs would they be selling.

And thus the birth of a ? of the day. I've been writing such questions for thirty-plus years as a daily challenge appended to my e-mail — and post on various social media, as well.

The English language is a prime source for such rhetorical questions, puns and frivolous thoughts. There is a seemingly endless number of words which are written identically yet have individual meanings. I suppose you realize that

Ed Kaiser

you can have brush in your yard, brush your teeth as well as brush up for a test. Yet I don't suppose you've ever asked a friend if they got a knot in their stomach when they tied the knot with their spouse under the knot in the big oak tree while the boat went by at ten knots.

Another fabulous source for thoughts that have me *Stumped* are common sayings. I suppose it depends on your mood whether your opponent has a fat chance or slim chance of winning. One of my favorite English oversights…or should I say shortsighted English…is we have to choose between give in, give out, or give up, but does anyone ever give down.

Such rhetorically humorous questions have intrigued me since my adolescent

STUMPED

years. Parking on driveways yet driving on parkways is a frivolous question that has probably been around since the Model-T needed a place to park. Most of the questions in this book originated in my own mind, yet I must admit that not all come entirely and only from my convoluted brain cells. Some ideas are transplanted in my head by friends or are random seeds scattered about the internet. I nurture those seeds into succinct punny phrasing.

So, whether originating in my mind or sprouting from weedy seeds, I offer all of these questions to give you pause to wonder how to answer them. I certainly hope you enjoy reading these questions which have me STUMPED. I also hope you think of me as a wise man, not a wise guy.

Ed Kaiser

STUMPED

Questions

A farmer can produce produce, but can he teach a sow to sow?

A stitch in time saves nine what?

AA, AAA, C, D… is that because the B was Neveready?

After you let the cat out of the bag, how do you get the miserable animal back in it?

Ed Kaiser

And just what good is cake
if you can't eat it too?

Are cultured people more like pearls
or bacteria?

Are dog biscuits made with
Collieflour?

Are electricians delighted when
they retire?

Are hard boiled eggs hard to beat?

STUMPED

Are puns for kids or just groan-ups?

Are pushing your luck and someone's button, simultaneous depressions?

Are retired cowboys deranged?

Are seatbelts as confining as wheelchairs?

Are the whole nine yards linear, square or cubic?

Ed Kaiser

Are you at that age when "happy hour" is a nap?

Are you chalant before or after being nonchalant?

Are you in the statistical mean if you mean to be mean?

Before Edison, what did a cartoonist use to signify a bright idea?

Can CIA agents be de-spysed?

STUMPED

Can forbidden fruits create a jam?

Can someone relying on horse sense
become an old nag?

Can the junk man refuse refuse?

Can you be too close to close
the door?

Can you can hide, or should you hide
it in the waste can?

Ed Kaiser

Can you explain how Noah went 40,
hot, muggy nights and never slapped
the mosquitoes?

Can you put down a book
on antigravity?

Can you upstage a play on words?

Chop a tree down…then chop it up?

Could an earthquake in DC be
attributed to the government's fault?

STUMPED

Could an optometrist see the apple of my eye?

Could crop circles be the work of a cereal killer?

Could we call a cows udder, a calfeteria?

Did "eavesdrop" have its origin in the drip involved or from the gutter it landed in?

Did Adam have a belly button?

Ed Kaiser

Did Cinderella need to "break in" her new glass slippers?

Did draft dodgers ever get caught in a cross wind?

Did hamburger ever have ham in it?

Did King Arthur ever have sleepless knights?

Did mythological sirens even have sirens?

STUMPED

Did Noah keep the bees in
his archives?

Did the "Little Mermaid" wear
an algaebra?

Did you hear about the row in the
row of oarsmen about how to row?

Did you know there are more
airplanes in the ocean than
submarines in the sky?

Didn't 6-Up have enough fizz?

Ed Kaiser

Do accountants ever lose their balance?

Do does like what a buck does?

Do egotistic people get me-deep in conversation?

Do ghost ships sail with skeleton crews?

Do holier-than-thou people have an altar ego?

STUMPED

Do I have to look through the whole box of animal crackers to see if the seal is broken?

Do meteorologists ever look outside when they predict the chance of rain "today"?

Do midwives help people out?

Do misers sit and watch the world go buy?

Ed Kaiser

Do old sailors get a little dinghy when they retire?

Do people in zero gravity rise in love?

Do sacred cows make the best hamburger?

Do some Terriers get
Scotch tape worms?

Do they remove all the grass from the yard of a Drug Rehab center?

STUMPED

Do we always have to make amends;
can't a person make just one amend?

Do witches use a spell checker?

Do women curl up and dye at a
Beauty Salon?

Do ya suppose what da bullfighters do
is avoidabull?

Do you ever get tired while
jogging your memory?

Ed Kaiser

Do you ever really rest in a restroom?

Do you often resent e-mail that someone resent?

Do you pull a mussel when you eat clams?

Do you think it's significant that there are ladybugs yet no gentlemanbugs?

Does a bicycle need a kick stand because it's two tired?

STUMPED

Does a hypochondriac try to out-smart their friends?

Does anyone ever mail in for a list of the sweepstakes winners?

Does anyone outside the British Commonwealth understand "penny wise, but pound foolish"?

Does England's Liverpool also have a kidney bank?

Ed Kaiser

Does gravitation affect falling in love?

Does killing time lengthen eternity?

Does the name Pavlov ring a bell?

Doesn't a person who's all thumbs
need a hand?

Doesn't it seem a bit risky to invest
your money with someone called
a broker?

STUMPED

Doesn't it seem a bit crossed up to say
our feet smell and our nose runs?

Doesn't Leap Year sound like we'd
skip over a day rather than add one?

Don't most parade "Floats" actually
look like they would sink?

Don't boxers actually fight in squares?

During baking, what does
shortening decrease?

Ed Kaiser

Duz hookt on fonix reely werk
four enkneewon?

Even if the masculine product is made
from the same material, why are they
not referred to as nylons?

Even if you're sensitive to gluten, can
you still feel your oats?

Has your mind ever wandered and
forgot to come home?

STUMPED

Has your train of thought
ever derailed?

Have you ever heard of caboodle
associated with anything other
than kit?

Have you ever snarled when traffic
is snarled?

Have you ever told someone to
"watch in" ?

Ed Kaiser

Have you ever wondered why down goes down very slow, while sloe goes down much faster?

How can slow down mean the same thing as slow up?

How can you help someone out, if you don't know where they came in?

How come there is neither pine nor apple in pineapple?

STUMPED

How could an atheist make an "act of God" claim against his insurance?

How could any envelope be smart enough to be self addressed?

How did a fool and his money get together in the first place?

How has inflation effected passing the buck?

Ed Kaiser

How important does a person have to be before they are considered assassinated instead of just murdered?

If "seconds" are the 2nd division of an hour, why aren't the minutes called "firsts"?

If you crossed Poison Ivy and Four-leaf Clover, would you get a rash of good luck?

If a mosquito bites a person taking a blood thinner, does it get diarrhea?

STUMPED

If a pathological liar says he is, is he?

If a pig loses its voice,
is it disgruntled?

If a plane banks into a bank, would it
bank off or bank on, the building?

If a principal loses his faculties,
should he retire?

If at first you don't succeed…,
shouldn't you at least try doing it like
your wife suggested?

Ed Kaiser

If Barbie is so popular, why do you have to buy her friends?

If flying is so safe, why do we depart from a terminal?

If I don't repeat myself, am I just being dundant?

If ignorance is bliss, why aren't more people happy?

If Jimmy cracks corn but nobody cares, why is there a song about him?

STUMPED

If Love is blind, why is lingerie so popular?

If love is blind, why is marriage a real eye-opener?

If one is to get revenge, does one have to get venge first?

If Pandas and Koalas are not truly bears, what do they do in the woods?

If pro is the opposite of con, what's the opposite of progress?

Ed Kaiser

If Satan lost his hair, would there be hell toupee?

If something is "to die for", isn't trying to get it self-defeating?

If the dove dove into the bush, was he bushed?

If the plan for the first drawing board didn't work out, what did they go back to?

STUMPED

If the sky is clear during the day, it's sunny; so if it's clear at night, shouldn't it be moony?

If the sky's the limit,
what's outer space?

If they're adders,
how do snakes multiply?

If you are resigned to resign,
why resign the contract?

Ed Kaiser

If you borrow money from a pessimist,
why give their money back?

If you break your nose while running
amok, will you smell funny?

If you don't drink shampoo,
how can it give you extra body?

If you don't pay your exorcist,
will you get repossessed?

If you fall asleep on your watch,
will you have to face time?

STUMPED

If you push the envelope,
isn't it still stationery?

If you try to fail... and succeed,
which have you actually done?

If you're in Cahoots, wouldn't you be
better off if you were in Cognito?

If you're not tense, are you past tense
or under pretense?

If you're not on a roll when it's called
up yonder, are you in a jam?

Ed Kaiser

In France, do they say
"pardon my English"
when excusing offensive language?

Is "I do" a short or long sentence?

Is a "wrong number" ever busy?

Is a book on voyeurism
a peeping tome?

Is a deflated spare tire the same
as a flat ab?

STUMPED

Is a Freudian slip when you say one thing and mean your mother?

Is a hangover the wrath of grapes?

Is a metronome a city-dwelling dwarf?

Is a minor collision of birds, just a feather bender?

Is a person getting ready to see the dentist, brushing up for an oral exam?

Ed Kaiser

Is a pessimist's blood type b-negative?

Is a radiator repair shop the best place to take a leak?

Is a shirt-tail relative one who needs to be tucked in?

Is a streaker suited for his job?

Is a tear too wet to tear in two?

STUMPED

Is a turtle without a shell homeless
or naked?

Is Atheism a non-prophet
organization?

Is Cinco de Mayo a day to remember
the demise of a ship laden
with Mayonnaise?

Is debacle at the end of da belt?

Is dreaming in color a pigment of
your imagination?

Ed Kaiser

Is fighting for peace oxymoronic
or just moronic?

Is giving someone a high five being
high-handed?

Is it because light travels faster than
sound, that some people appear bright
until you hear them speak?

Is it better to be in time,
not just on it?

STUMPED

Is it easier to see the pie in the sky if you're pie-eyed?

Is it just tennis players who think love means nothing?

Is it possible four an electronic proof reeder too air?

Is it right to slug a snail?

Is it sexual discrimination that there are no meter butlers?

Ed Kaiser

Is it true that cannibals don't eat
clowns because they taste funny?

Is Marx's tomb a communist plot?

Is Sam Hill a person or a place?

Is sexual harassment ever a problem
for the self-employed?

Is there a tax on the wages of sin?

STUMPED

Isn't "Free Gift" redundant?

Isn't a permanent really a temporary?

Isn't a word to the wise unnecessary?

Isn't everything in the last place we'd look for it?

Isn't it counterproductive to "Honk if you want Peace"?

Ed Kaiser

Isn't it the fiddler, not the fiddle itself, that's fit?

Isn't the phrase "back and forth" backward?

Isn't there something redundant about "PIN number"?

Isn't won ton an awful lot of soup?

Isn't "Civil War" oxymoronic?

STUMPED

Isn't it a bit unnerving that doctors call what they do a "practice"?

Johann Bach wasn't wealthy but was he baroque?

Just where does a bank expect to get an "insufficient funds" fee from?

Should the Energizer Bunny be arrested and charged with battery?

Should you believe someone who says you're gullible?

Ed Kaiser

Should you desert dessert in
the desert?

Should you put a dog house
on a lot of trouble?

Should you use a car or a hammer to
drive a hard bargain?

Should you wear safety shoes
when you mow the lawn
if you're lack-toes intolerant?

Shouldn't chili be called hottie?

STUMPED

Shouldn't the Air and Space Museum be empty?

So, is anyone minding their own r's and s's?

The recipe states to preheat the oven… Isn't pre-heat and cold about the same?

They don't just go up, so why call them escalators?

Two bits…singular or plural?

Ed Kaiser

Well…, if I were you…
who'd be me?

What are you fishing for when you
cast an aspersion?

What came first orange or the color?

What do they mean, "Extra Virgin"
olive oil? Isn't virginity an absolute?

What happens if a cow loses
her whey?

STUMPED

What if the Hokey Pokey IS what it's all about?

What wire did I just get in under?

What's so tough about cutting mustard?

What's the best time for a snipe hunt?

What's the difference between a hissie fit and a conniption?

Ed Kaiser

What's the difference between
flammable and inflammable?

When all is said and done...is there
more said than done?

When madness takes its toll,
do you need exact change?

When someone gets too big for
their britches, will they be exposed
in the end?

STUMPED

When the lights out you can't see them, so why do we say the stars are out?

When we elect a female president, will her husband be the first gentleman?

When you are dog tired at night, could it be that you've growled all day long?

When you buy navel oranges, should you look for innies or outies?

Ed Kaiser

When you egg someone on,
could you get egg on your face?

When you're in over your head,
should you keep your mouth shut?

When you've had enough,
isn't it too late to call your uncle?

Where in the nursery rhyme does it
say humpty dumpty is an egg?

Where is the zerk for
elbow grease located?

STUMPED

Which do you do most often,
spin yarn or spin a yarn?

Which requires more effort; holding
your tongue or picking up the pieces?

Which takes more strength; holding a
grudge or your tongue?

Who actually cans the worms we're
not supposed to open?

Who decided that cleave should mean
both stick together and split apart?

Ed Kaiser

Who decided that Little Rock
sounded better than
Big Stone, Arkansas?

Who thought that "Firefly" was an
appropriate name for a beetle?

Who was Jack and why was his
jumping so remarkable?

Why are overlook and oversee
so different?

STUMPED

Why are they called tug boats when they usually push?

Why aren't there "starboardholes"?

Why ask to borrow a Kleenex… you don't intend to return it, do you?

Why did kamikazes wear helmets?

Why do so many people interrupt when something "speaks for itself"?

Ed Kaiser

Why do they lock gas station bathrooms...what's in there worth stealing?

Why do we bake cookies but cook bacon?

Why do we call them ice cubes when they are rarely shaped that way?

Why do we feel it necessary to tell someone when we're speechless?

STUMPED

Why do we heat our homes to a higher temperature than we cool to in the summer?

Why do we make lemonade with artificial flavoring and furniture polish with real lemons?

Why do we park in driveways and drive on parkways?

Why do we put suits in a garment bag and garments in a suitcase?

Ed Kaiser

Why do we say the alarm goes off… doesn't it actually go on?

Why do we say we've "slept like a baby" when they wake up every two hours?

Why do you have to jump to conclusions…can't you just blindly walk into them?

Why does Goofy stand erect yet Pluto walks on all four legs?

STUMPED

Why doesn't a storm die up when the rain lets down?

Why don't we coach our kids to say "Hi, Hi" like we do "bye, bye"?

Why don't we spell phonetic the way it sounds?

Why don't you ever see the headline: "Psychic Wins Lottery"?

Why fix dinner…it's not broken, is it?

Ed Kaiser

Why is it called tourist season
if we can't shoot them?

Why is it that fixing a car and fixing a
fight have opposite applications?

Why is it that humans, but not
machines, can be off and running?

Why is it that so many people want to
feed your pet peeve?

Why is it that we recite at plays
and play at recitals?

STUMPED

Why is it that when a door is open, it's ajar, yet when a jar is open, it's not adoor?

Why is it that you buy one onion, cut it up, put it on food and suddenly you have onions?

Why is it; when you transport something by car it is a shipment, yet the same thing sent by ship is cargo?

Why is the X a hug…or is it the O?

Ed Kaiser

Why is there an expiration date on Sour Cream?

Why isn't popped corn considered a vegetable?

Why isn't the number 11 pronounced onety one?

Why isn't trimming the Christmas tree like trimming the hedge?

Why paramedics…won't one suffice?

STUMPED

Why try to win the battle of the sexes when it's so much fun to fraternize with the enemy?

Why would a cat be interested in anyone's tongue?

Will a dyslexic walk into a bra?

Will a lot of kneeling keep you in good standing?

Will a phew eggs make a stink bomb?

Ed Kaiser

Will an Easter bonnet cover
a wild hare?

Will antipasto negate eating pasta?

Will it help to be off the wall when
you feel up against the wall?

Will space travel give new meaning to
ice cream floats?

Will you dye when gray hairs appear?

STUMPED

Will you ever hear the end of it,
if you break wind in an echo chamber?

Without an abundance of money, how am I supposed to know if it can't buy me happiness?

Without pupils, can a teacher see?

Would a customer beef if the farmer beefed up the beef?

Would a fly without wings be called a walk?

Ed Kaiser

Would you call an athlete with a peanut allergy an anaphylactic jock?

Would you consider Velcro a rip-off?

Would a 12-step program for non-stop talkers, be called OnAndOnAnon?

Wouldn't it be safer if rams used their butt to butt?

STUMPED

Would an eye doctor on an Alaskan
island be considered an
optical Aleutian?

STUMPED

Questions with Answers

Is the jam we need help getting out of,
made from the pickle we got into?

Yup, called blueberry relish.

If money doesn't grow on trees,
why do banks have branches?

*You're definitely getting close to the root
of the problem, but sadly,
I'm going to have to leave.*

*So that they can go out on a limb
to loan saps money.*

Ed Kaiser

If a baker kneads something, does he stand in a bread line?

*Only if he needs bread...
like money, dude.*

Isn't it detrimental to give someone a piece of your mind?

Not if they promise to give it back.

If a cow won't give milk, is it a Milk Dud?

*That's udder nonsense.
I might even say that it's bull.*

STUMPED

Do lame ducks become sitting ducks?
Only when they can no longer stand it.

Would a procrastinator's self help group ever meet?
I can't answer this question today.
Let me get back to you on that.
One of these days we certainly will.
Of course, just not today.
Perhaps tomorrow.

Won't a little flexibility keep you from getting bent out of shape?
Or could it be that flexibility allows you to get bent out of shape more easily?

Ed Kaiser

Does he who passes gas in church, sit in his own pew?
I would say the answer is rather alimentary.

How do you get down from an elephant?
You don't. You get down from a duck.
Maybe he has a rope hidden in his trunk.
Fall.
You get down from a goose.

Is drilling for oil, boring?
I'd have to know the hole story to answer this.

STUMPED

Is it safe to say that the guy who invented the Hay-baler made a bundle?

He was absolutely raking it in.

Sadly, though, he was only grasping at straws.

They are making mounds now.

And stacking up the green.

They could be rolling in dough.

When an agnostic dies, does he go to the "great perhaps"?

I doubt it.

I can't say for sure either way.

He goes to the great flaming "Now you know".

Ed Kaiser

What general direction is cattywumpus?

Cattywampus still works, but it's half a bubble off plumb. Which is still better than being discombobulated.

80 degrees from higgledy-piggledy.

Should we skirt or be a defender of the issue of fenders no longer getting skirts?

You couldn't have asked a bumpier question. I'll have to hood my answer.

If someone wants to talk turkey, could you end up eating crow?

You could but forget the talk, I would eat the turkey.

STUMPED

Supposedly, diamonds are a girl's best friend…why does a man have to settle for a dog?

'Cause that's all you will cuddle with until I get my diamond. (from woman)

That's just the way it is. (from woman)

The dog can't talk back.

What does vice have to do with versa?

Versa can never be trusted… rap sheet a mile long.

Should you arrest a dog for littering?

There are ways to permanently arrest her from ever littering again.

Ed Kaiser

Is "Roe versus Wade" the
dilemma Washington faced before
crossing the Delaware?

I don't think "Wade" was a viable choice.

*Maybe not, but you could say he made a
Supreme decision to Roe.*

Will the tennis racket ever
end up in court?

*Yes! They usually are tried
in pairs though.*

Yes…I believe the players serve time.

*Yes, because the net result is
love at first lob.*

STUMPED

If you swallow your pride,
will your stomach roar?

I'd be lion if I said no.

When the lights go out,
do they have a favorite spot?

*No. Spot lights do not go out as often
as others.*

If you mixed Milk of Magnesia,
Orange Juice and Vodka would you
have a Phillips Screwdriver?

*Not a drink that a bartender would serve
a REGULAR customer.*

Ed Kaiser

Does the rabbit think his foot
is lucky?
Just his back foot.

Can someone tell me why I have this
string on my finger?
This seems to be a common thread...
Sorry, I forgot.

What went wrong with Preparations
A through G?
Some things just didn't work out.

STUMPED

Are you plum out of luck looking for plums in plum pudding?

I would expect so, but don't want to be raisin false hope.

Field corn…really? Where else would you grow corn but in a field?

If you were on your toes, you might have suggested that location for growing corns.

In Feudalism, does your count vote?

It would be an exercise in feudality.

Ed Kaiser

Shouldn't night time events be considered "after light"?

On a school night, it could be "after math".

Even if you're willing to compile lots of data, is graphing where you draw the line?

Perhaps it's where you step up to the bar.

Does going to the bathroom always require going to the bathroom?

Perhaps you could come up with descriptors through the process of elimination.

STUMPED

Does the "Grapevine" create more sour grapes than sweet ones?

It just depends if the grapes make wine or whine.

Why "English Muffin" when it originated in Boston and looks more like a stepped-on bagel than a muffin?

Because we beat the English into submission, and ever since then their muffins have been flat!

If a chicken coop has four doors, shouldn't it be considered a sedan?

[Yes, I know, this is only valid as a verbalized question]

Ed Kaiser

If a tree falls in the forest and no one is around to see it, …do the other trees make fun of it?

No, they leaf it alone! I went out on a limb to say that.

No they don't make fun of it. They already know it is a Sap.

When a tree falls in the forest you will probably see the root of the problem.

Will fish, in de school, take debate?

Only if it's a bookworm!
Only if it thinks it can rebutt!

STUMPED

Do Lipton employees dare to take a coffee break?

Better yet what do Maxwell House employees drink with their crumpets?

If they drink anything that's not good to the last drop, it's likely grounds for termination.

Folgers is wrong; the best part of waking up is crawling back in bed after you pee.

Do two physicians make a paradox?

Do two medics make a paramedics?

If those two doctors each buy a boat, they will need a pair o' docks.

Do they have to wear dockers?

Ed Kaiser

We can "give out", "give in" and "give up"…what happened to "give down"?

What about "give back"?

There is no "give front".

Did Dr. Jekyll ever really feel like himself?

Well, he did try to Hyde a lot of his problems.

If the corn farmer fires his workers, will they stalk him?

There's a kernel of truth here.

Probably. He'd better keep his ears open.

STUMPED

If two silk worms raced,
would they end up in a tie?
Better than making a run in a stocking.
That's a knotty problem.
Maybe in Windsor.
More like a tie-die!

Will the calves of my legs eat the
corn on my toe?
Hard to say; maybe if they knuckle down.

If she becomes a whiskey maker,
will he love her still?
Hard to prohibit such a spirit.
Sounds like she'd be quite a corker!
"Vat do you mean?" asked Helga.

Ed Kaiser

If you're in the lead,
could carrying lead lead to defeat?

*It depends upon the condition of defeat.
Depends on how big your lead with lead is.*

Why does fat chance and slim chance mean the same thing?

It doesn't. Apparently as slim chance is cited as the preferred alternative to none, fat chance is the most preferred, since you don't hear anybody saying somebody's chances are fat to none.

On a clock, isn't the second hand really the third one?

First, give me a second.

STUMPED

Is there any sound coming from
the hoarse chorale?

Neigh.

Why waste your breath calling a cat?

Just turn on the electric can opener.

Is Acupuncture just a jab well done?

More like a stab in the dark.

*Just someone trying to get their
point across.*

Ed Kaiser

If you've been out of sorts,
do you remember going in?

*I just tell Judy when I'm out of sorts, and
she goes to the store to get some more.*

Can you ever be sure you're indecisive?

I'm confused. No wait! Maybe I'm not.

Would you be in Seine,
if you jumped off a bridge in Paris?

Or in Egypt, I could be in denial.
*If you jump in to the Seine you may
Rue de Day.*

STUMPED

Would you bring suit if your
new suit didn't suit you?

My tailor pleats not guilty.

Why do we say "tuna fish"
but not "beef mammal"?

*Because if we didn't call it a fish we
would confuse it with a chicken of the sea.*

Do you start or stop something
when you wind it up?

*Some people wind up a toy when done
playing so it is all ready to go next time.*

*Others wait and wind it up
just before they start.*

Ed Kaiser

Why isn't shortening the opposite
of longing?

That's a lard question.

Were chastity belts
labor-saving devices?

*No woman in those days could ever
conceive of wearing one.*

Inconceivable.

If someone is average,
are they necessarily mean?

Only sum of the time.

STUMPED

Where can I get some illegal size pads of paper?

Psst—meet me at the guard shack at the tracks by Hawk Island. 10:30 tonight. Flash your lights 3 times. Two long and one short. Small unmarked bills only.

Isn't your bottom actually closer to the middle?

Unless you have furniture disease (that's when your chest has fallen into your drawers).

If a store displays bar stools, do you consider them as stool samples?

Urine the right ballpark.

Ed Kaiser

Why do we take minutes at a meeting that wastes hours?

Hmmm, I don't recall you ever being at our bored meeting.

Will lox on your bagel protect it from thievery?

I don't know, but it sounds fishy.

If you give it your awl, how could you be boring?

Only if you continue to push on through.

That's a piercing question.

STUMPED

If opposites attract, how come birds of a feather flock together?

I suppose it's their birds eye view.

Do you think Johann ever said he'd be Bach in a minuet?

If he did, it would have been with a Lohengrin!

I don't think he could Handel that.

Sure, just as good as another Johann could Pachelbel in a box.

If he didn't he would surely have been baroque.

With or without the Monet?

Ed Kaiser

What part of "part with part of a part" don't you understand?
The question departed my brain before I could impart the answer.

At what age does a man's wild oats become All Bran?
One year this side of senility.
Sow what?

Where is cloud nine in relation to seventh heaven?
Two levels below.
Heading upwards…7, 9, rapture.

STUMPED

How does being full of beans
put egg on your face?

Usually because someone eggs you on.
If you go bananas, that could do it.

Does going to pot mean the same
today as a hundred years ago?

Seems about as different as a going to a
joint back then and smoking one now.

What's behind every
successful woman?

That's for them to know and
men to wonder about.

A "herstory" of persistence
That's it…behind.

Ed Kaiser

Data is or Data are?
Data are plural…yet some data is secure.

Are the wurst jokes about sausage?
Not if you de-liver them right.

Are cannibals fed up with people?
Just those on South Beach.

Does a book about espionage need a cover?
Yes, but it must be a secret, so nobody knows.

Who needs rhetorical questions?
You bought the book, I guess you do.

Ed Kaiser

To order additional copies of Stumped, please send $15.00 (book price plus shipping and handling) to Buttonwood Press, P.O. Box 716, Haslett, MI 48840. Make check payable to Buttonwood Press. To order multiple copies please contact Buttonwood Press at info@buttonwoodpress.com